Written in Blood

Post-Modern
Penitentiary Poetry

Written in Blood

Post-Modern
Penitentiary Poetry

Jon-Darren

HenschelHAUS Publishing, Inc.
Milwaukee, Wisconsin

Published by HenschelHAUS Publishing, Inc.
www.henschelHAUSbooks.com

ISBN: 978159598-545-3
E-ISBN: 978159598-546-0
Audio ISBN: 978159598-547-7
LCCN: 2017941431

Cover design by DarRen Morris

A portion of the proceeds from the sales of this book
is dedicated to Ye Are Gods Ministry

Printed in the United States of America.

To my mom and dad

Table of Contents

ONTOLOGY/PSYCHOLOGY/SPIRITUALITY

Preface

This collection of poems is a commentary about my life, how I view the world as someone who is not fully integrated into society, and the reasons this is true for me and others who embody similar circumstances.

I have frequently felt neglected, forgotten and voiceless. Some of the adverse consequences I have experienced are the result of poor choices; other are due to purposeful disenfranchisement, marginalization of the economically depressed, and a desire by the global power structure to maintain a culture of whiteness.

While incarcerated, I began to write as a means of contemplation and personal examination. This turned into a passion that has now allowed me to speak truth and champion the plight of others plagued by forces intent on destroying them as well. This work is a candid view of the government, churches, correctional institutions, relationships, and the soul.

To see me in my brokenness and subsequent triumphs is to see our society in the same light. This book is my attempt to expose wrongs and injustice in an effort to promote truth and equality for all people.

—Jon-Darren

Socioeconomic/Political Essay

The socioeconomic situation of poor people and, specifically, Blacks in America is based on an inequality of justice coupled with a lack of political power. If Jesus is alive, in us and this purportedly Christian nation, we need a true conversion to testify that, in the land of the free and the home of the brave, we are all free.

The poems in this section grasp the political climate and milieu of the time and what must be done. The people have been fooled to believe terrorist only strap explosives to their bodies and blow up planes, when they also sponsor regime change through overt and clandestine means, siphon resources from the Developing World, and subjugate the people they claim to help through guile and lies from Paris to Pakistan.

The turn of events, from a decrease in crime to an increase in prisons, gave rise to a subset of the population who has become perennial victims—directly and latently. Due to deficiency and misuse of political power, Black and poor people are reactionary. Mental prisons of consumerism, materialism, and self-hate contribute to failed policies. As we revolt with dollars and our bodies, by living out the Quran and the Bible, we will rebuild our neighborhoods by providing for self through ownership of land and the means of production.

As evidenced from the "Black Lives Matter" movement and the 20th anniversary of the Million Man March, young people are tired of the status quo and are making changes. The unfettered truth springs from the mouth of babes and this new Joshua Generation. If we continue to push an agenda of mendacity and complacency, we will fail our progeny and usher in the next, new Jim Crow.

Due to neglect of love and understanding, our economic, political, and social systems are in ruins. Black people have allowed our minds, children, dollars, and communities to be locked in a mental complex. While de jure slavery has been over for 150 years, the questions I ask, and attempt to answer, are who's free and whose free have we attained or aspired to achieve in that time?

Justice Inequality

If Freddie Gray lived, he'd be in Jessup
the New Jim Crow still saying, "Yes Sum."
Lynched Sandra Bland hung her high
crucified Tamar Rice made us all cry

From Mike Brown to Eric Garner police brutality
don't accept violence from them you pay they salary
They lock up Black bodies because most are silent
scared middle-class people that makes you compliant

Brothers go to prison, they should go to college
classrooms are concentration camps there is no knowledge
From slavery to Black Codes, Jim Crow, civil rights
Black people are you tired being killed? Then unite!

Lobby your Congresswoman instead of Vera Wang
spending your money to look good you should be ashamed
Clean yourself up by tearing down systemic racism
they lock minorities up and make salaries on recidivism

The game is flawed, this we all know
more time for crack than soft powdered snow
They locked up two generations instead of giving them jobs
blame NAFTA and Bill Clinton whom we thought was God

The prison industrial complex will continue to subsist
as long as we the people don't insist
on equal justice for Brown and Black men
if we ain't all free we all locked up then

8:55 AM CST
9-11-2015

Jesus Ain't Dead

Jesus ain't dead he at Clinton Correctional
got laced for a rape in '93 no DNA
spending time gambling slowly wasting away
codefendant walked, judge said someone must pay

Jesus' dead he biddin' at Statesville
took the murder charge for the prince
said they had his family they ain't got 15 cents
plead guilty, went away, permanently behind a fence

Jesus ain't dead he up in Jessup
caught 30 for two robberies in PG
the streets loved him but ain't sent no TV
started banging heroin in the joint done caught Hep C

Jesus still being crucified up in Green Bay
three home invasions, false imprisonment, and kidnap
40 better than a L, luckily the gun jammed—good mishap
ain't fuck nothing but gotta register as a sex offender—fuck that

Jesus still being crucified in San Quentin
beat the snot out of that CO three years in the SHU
guard definitely deserved it you know what they do
then they lied about—intimidation—pigs stick together like glue

Jesus still being crucified out in Leavenworth
wire fraud, criminal enterprising, knocked wit' ten keys
mama wouldn't tell got twenty for conspiracy
it's crazy he rolled on her and got 5 she the real G

Jesus ain't dead He's talking through me
resurrected, conscience; devils scared I am He
let my people go we'll make it Pell Grant or not
when those locked up or have been unite, we can't be stopped

9:50 AM CST
7-30-2015

Conversion

Saul went to Tuskegee
he wore Gucci and rode BMW
told Black men to adhere to the law
teaching capitalism and neo-colonialism

The people heard of his authority
he told poor women to get off welfare
go to church—not his—and repent
teaching conservative values

One day he was robbed
shot in the head
he was blinded for weeks
homeless lesbians laid healing hands on him

He saw the light of Truth
something like scales fell from his eyes
the Savior touched him
christened him Jamaal

Jamaal went to St. Louis and Oakland
he wore dashikis and carried a pitcher of water
told Black men to fight white supremacy
teaching liberation through cooperation

The master was frightened by his authority
he told poor women to plant gardens
be the church—with him—and reap dividends of blessings
teaching love for self and protection of family

One day they imprisoned him
beat him like Emmitt Till
he was in the hole for weeks
racist, homosexual guards sodomized him

He saw the darkness of humanity
something like hate filled his heart
retribution touched his soul
baptized him in revolution

unknown time
unknown date

In the Land of the Free
and the Home of the Brave

In the land of the free and the home of the brave
White children are rambunctious
Black children are pathologized
White men are assertive
Black men are aggressive
White women are sexy
Black women are hoes

In the land of the free and the home of the brave
White children get warned
Black children get arrested
White men get probation
Black men get prison
White women get praised
Black women get hung

In the land of the free and the home of the brave
White children have tablets
Black children have chalk
White men have leisure
Black men have indolence
White women have careers
Black women have jobs

In the land of the free and the home of the brave
Inordinate credence placed on skin
Game determines your lot and dividends
Uncle Sam is calculating and scheming
White domination is the result and the meaning

7:25 PM CST
9-29-2015

Real Middle East Terrorist

US not in Afghanistan to bring about democracy
Uncle Sam got boys dying for them poppy seeds
Islamic State is there selling dope too
Blaspheming the name of Allah bringing heroin through

Taking over countries not because they infidels
Truth of America is desire for dope and oil wells
Bush and Company in bed with the bin Laden family
Mostly Saudis brought them towers down not no Iraqis

Red, white, and blue regime never seeks to be peaceful
20% of the budget spent on war because they evil
Fought a proxy war with Russia in 1980
The shah was gone so Hussein became our baby

Killed him and his kids because he was willful
He can gas Kurds, but no playing with the billfold
Killed Qaddafi because he wanted a United States of Africa
China want they resources and world domination the US is after

The bald eagle in Saudi Arabia and Kuwait
America hates Assad, but Putin pulled rank
Very soon Lady Liberty won't control it all
Because like Rome and Greece, this white supremacist
    empire will fall

12:20 PM CST
10-16-2015

Train to Paris

El Khazzani was subdued by two whites and
  one who appeared Black
at least two niggas on a train to Paris—imagine that
In the West on Friday when you apprehend and hogtie a Negro
Monday you get the French Medal of Honor—obviously a hero

Not that he wasn't wrong for wanting to destroy
It's the manner of the method he chose to employ
Lone wolf terrorist are created through injustice
indict they system; the Patriot Act is suspect

Nothing happens in a vacuum except suffocating death
life is breathed into marginalization-filled threats
You'll be forgotten and broke if you fight to get conscience
no chance to become president or graduate from college

Terrorism is the mother of America and lying is her dad
enslaved, subjugated, and killed the Indigenous like mad
Poor whites and some Muslims have been shut out too
these people aren't crazy, they're returning your due

12:50 PM CST
8-30-2015

Turn of Events

Mad at me cause I don't do five for 20
I need all my money, ain't a damn thing funny
Now it's '96 and it's time to check my crack house
got a whole brick and my boy Big Roy is back out

I'm down at the lake shining hard on 100s
hoes see me looking good at Van Domes—they want it
New millennium, new game—credit card fraud
my bitch selling dro, niggas on the Trays ballin real hard

I'm still reppin' the Deuces 2-6 all day
riding flats on skinnys it's '06 I do it my way
Took a trip down to Texas to get 20 bricks
my mans work for the people, but I don't know that shit

I go take the trip wit' Roy he out on parole
they only had 10 I bought out they whole store
Coming through Oklahoma checkpoint search the car
I'm knocked 10 thangs, 250K no more trap star

"Who is your supplier?" I don't say shit
They show me pics off the wire; my man's is a bitch
Had me come down to the 713 big mini mansion
    and you police?
They ask again, "You feel like dancing?"

I bust some heads in the Chi, plea for 10 wit' no trial
he told on me, I got you, and now I'm back out
I'm coming out the bar and my pistol is tucked
lil' dawg look familiar, but pills got me all fucked

"Break yo self School," is all I remember
turned around gave 'um 13—coldest day in December
Now I'm back in a cell and it's Victim Impact Week
All my life victimized, my daddy was killed dead in the street

Unknown time
Unknown date

Who's the Victim?

Who is the victim, what about me?
Got me locked in a cage 13-inch TV
This little ass flat screen cost 300 bucks
They got 40, 50 inches don't cost that much

The so-called victim is dead, but I'm stuck in a cell
That nigga deserved 13 shots, sent him right to hell
Tried to rob me, he won't pull that no mo'
May he rest in piss, thank you 4-4

This mattress hard and bugs fall from the ceiling
COs talking shit, the warden talking about healing
"Concentrate on your victim; what about the community?"
Ya'll shoulda thought about that before you
        pumped drugs on 21st street

My neighborhood was alright and people had jobs
And every man wasn't a doe boy or out stealing cars
Men were with women—no niggas and bitches
The stove was used for spaghetti not cooking them chickens

Then Nancy and Ronnie said it's a war on drugs
Dropping eggs in skillets, no warrant plant bugs
No-knock raid grandma shot dead
Wasn't no dope here, just a QP under the bed

Crack hoes infested with Chlamydia
Babies born with HIV—government getting rid of ya
Get less time for powder than rocks
Now I sell boy this shit must stop

The proliferation of prisons—industrial complex
No industry, no work so you know what's next
I get a half for 600 bag it up all nickels
Post up on the block—no shorts—hypes acting fickle

They say we want H, five points for fifty
I say, "I got grams for 80, no need to be persnickety!"
I'll get you high: weed, boy, or blow
I'm back out—fire sale—this shit must go

I'm getting some money and my PO on my ass
"If you get another ATR I'll lock you up fast."
My guy do lawn care so he cut me a check
That should keep Ms. Daisy from breathing down my neck

I'm shining real hard, 650 new coupe
My girl got a Jag, she missing a roof
We moved to Brookfield mortgage five stacks
This heroin moving, call me Mr. Brown Pack

I'm at the gas station my cellular vibrates
Lil' dawg say, "It's me, sorry fo' da wait."
Before I look up, I'm blocked in, they jump out
I hit the gas and floor it, gun shots no doubt

This nigga got me, lil dawg set me up
I'm bleeding out my face, blood pouring like a cup
Damn, what to do, can I make it to St. Joe's?
I'm fenna be dead, black snot coming out my nose

I hit a pole so I guess I'm dead on arrival
Truth is I'm not the shooter or the lone survivor
I'm the storyteller and I know it well
The killer is America, the victim Black males

4:38 PM CST
8-25-2015

Stop Spending

Systematic injustice keeps the people enslaved
Due to mass consumption are kids are raised in graves
Grave danger due to ideologies of materialism
Consumed by ideologues who encourage consumerism

$500 jeans and Gucci sneakers are cool
And the real fool is you who should pay tuition for school
Or if you was a revolutionary you'd make education free
You won't, too busy at Neiman's on a credit shopping spree

No intentions of paying it back, credit score stuck at 500
Your kids go to subpar schools and at clubs you pop bubbly
When is you gone go to a PTA meeting?
Instead of happy hour with machinations of cheating

Black, Brown, Red, Yellow, and poor white
Wake up, clean up your block, then unite
Stop going to malls and outlets spending your dollars
Invest in your community so our kids will have a tomorrow

12:15 PM CST
8-27-2015

Start Saving

What have Vera, Jimmy, or Ralph done for your family?
I'm assuming nothing, to be put bluntly not a damn thang
They in places called Malibu and ranches in Santa Barbara
While you stuck in hood hovels giving up hard-earned dollars

Please open an IRA at a Black-owned bank
Max out the employer contribution on your 401K
Pay down old bills to get your credit score up
Who wants to marry you when your credit is fucked?

Save 10% of your gross, forget about the preacher
He should be like Paul a real Christ teacher
Get ya bread up—four months of living expenses
Then learn about stocks and Black charitable giving

Save like a Jew, eat like a Muslim, get peace like a Buddhist
Start saving your mind by consuming less
If all you do is spend, shop, and ball
When you get old you'll have no money at all

11:32 AM CST
8-28-2015

Your Prisons Are Killing You

Your feet look pretty
Your mind is empty
Koreans do your nails
Black men rot in jails

Prisoner filled with potential
Prisons of mental differential
Jewish bankers take your money
Black men playing the dummy

Are you only able to sell drugs?
Are you aware the CIA is the plug?
Afghans grow poppies you kill for
Black man is America's whore

Killing you with materialism
Killing your kids with militarism
Mexicans are not our enemies
Black man you are still kin to me

You must now unite
You must get right
Africans are original man
Black man you need to understand

12:00 PM CST
8-23-2015

Surahs 2:96 and 9:97

All Jews ain't bad, all whites ain't good
but we need to kick Arabs out our neighborhood
Muslims live on the Southside and invade the North
come to my block and sell beer and pork

Ya whole life is haram, plus you dope date
sitting in gas stations selling roses and rape
our young girls and crack addicted women
they'd behead you at home, here you don't even get prison

Brothers who play for Jewish sports teams
take they money and make our neighborhoods clean
Instead of giving money back to they family
support Black banks and reinvest your salary

Time to get wise with our 1.6 trillion dollars
stop thinking as hood niggas and become ghetto scholars
Life is an economic jungle and Black people are the prey
besides collect offering mega-church preacher only say pray

Jews ain't never stopped sucking us dry
at they department stores overpriced clothes we buy
Jesus ain't the only one from Israel you bow down to
it seems like Obama is scared of Netanyahu

We must put our money where our mouth is
buying expensive clothes and don't have a mortgage
For Blacks to be respected we need capital and land
otherwise they'll hang us and make it out fault like Sandra Bland

10:55 AM CST
10-16-2015

Failed Policies

We tell people from Mexico get away
Those illegals from Eastern Europe we let stay
Work visas and green cards for Indians
Indigenous Amerindians we paint as savage red skins

You must meet the dream of the capitalist machine
Otherwise get behind the wall of Trump's nightmare regime
If you're Brown you're a rapist and cut my grass
If you're white you're just right and you get a pass

Country built on the backs of Blacks
Then they sublimated with Irish and Jews—don't forget that
Let in Italians and Germans to give them jobs
When the former slaves would have worked just as hard

Immigration to the US is about assimilation
Your color must pass the test for proper integration
We say we love Jesus and are Spirit filled
If I say Jesus is a Black savior do you accept him still?

Your Christ was a refuge in the Motherland
Fugitive family on the run—Christ on the lam
Jesus is still running from Sudan and Honduras
Your no humanitarian, you go to Cuba to be a tourist

People are fleeing effects of imperialist domination
No need of slaves, but what's under the ground in your nation
Oil, raw materials, marijuana, and wood
The West needs it all to look and feel good

Don't give us you tired or hungry, you keep them
We want your best and brightest like Carlos Slim
If you come to our shores be ready to swim
You are not the right color, toss her back in

Migrate to immigrate, once again wash and repeat
Miasma of lies allows America to live in defeat
If Jesus is our example and we're all American denizens
When they come, let them stay so they can become citizens

5:20 PM CST
9-10-2015

Niggas Too

White looking Natives don't empathize with Hispanics
They hate niggas too
Syrian refugees don't understand it
They hate niggas too
Croatinas here illegally, no one hunts them
They hate niggas too
Dominicans kick Haitians out—what a sin
They hate niggas too
Saudis fight proxy wars with Iranians
They hate niggas too
Mexicans who don't cut grass aren't our friends
They hate niggas too
Poor Caucasians, in tailors, feel good about whiteness
They hate niggas too
Laotian and Hmong killed in favor of ethnic cleanliness
They hate niggas too
Poor, disenfranchised people really hate themselves
Because they niggas too!

8:03 AM CST
9-17-2015

The Snow Falls Quietly

The snow falls quietly
concrete draped in whiteness
I see it from my cell
covering virulent jurisprudence

Incontrovertible parsimony of liberty
deleterious aberration of justice
enthralled by whiteness
the snow falls quietly

Abominable interruption of justice
the snow falls quietly
fulminations of rehabilitation are subterfuge
trepidation from whiteness

Axiomatic tocsin of whiteness
dissident trapped in consternation
the snow falls quietly
nefarious system that's seemingly irrepressible

12:14PM CST
2-02-2016

The People's Truth

Latino/Hispanic Heritage Month should be monthly,
But only a few of us are from Hispaniola
None of us are from a place called Latin
We speak the language of our colonizers

I come from the lineage of Montezuma
Strong Taino blood runs through my veins
We spoke Arawak not the Spanish of the enslaved
They lied to us in Brazil and gave us Portuguese

My people are strong, we are the Inca
We had charted the sky before Europeans
I don't come from cannibalistic savages
Aboriginals in the nation of the Maya were here first

God always loved us, we knew Her for millennia
She guided our course and fed us from the Earth
Then white men came with deadly diseases
Killed those who couldn't be captured

Now you say I can't cross a fake border
You exploit my labor in the maquiladora
My life is impoverished because of what you took
Instead of my ancestors, I'm confused, to Europe I look

Columbus was a murderer and a child molester
You've given him a country and a day
How can you discover millions of people?
Rename everything and give it back

Soon we will unite because we are the majority
We have become conscience of you—the minority
You are now on notice that I know my history
The lies you sold my people will haunt you

12:05 PM CST
9-13-2015

The Puzzle of True Love

I don't hate white people
I hate white supremacy
Ben Carson's polices hate me
Bernie Sanders understands the poor

Bill grew up around us
Don't mean he love us
All white people ain't bad
All Black people ain't good

Race in America is a puzzle
We have all the pieces
No one wants to join them
Blacks hate each other

Blacks must unite like Jews
Caucus like rich Caucasians
Open industries like Chinese
And truly love yourself

9:28 AM CST
11-25-2015

From the Mouths of Babes (Psalm 8:2)

Pants hanging low don't mean my IQ is
Music up loud don't mean I'm stupid
I watch the news, follow the Minister on Twitter
10.10.15 was hot, Million March don't quite remember

Don't insult or assault the intelligence of the youth
Growing up parents didn't care for your group
This generation will utilize the ankh
At solving society's problems we won't flunk

Police shoot us down for putting hands up
Obviously, no gun, my shirt is tucked
In $300 jeans mama worked overtime for
Rent ain't paid cause it's holes in the floor

Life is cut short no reason to save
Spend it all fast, premonitions of early graves
I guess I could be president or a CEO
But my school only promote violence and how to cook dope

They teach us to be inmates, not scholars
Security guards in blue constantly holler
"Get to class...Where is your pass?"
Then secretly feel on Teesha big ass

Daddy, how you gone teach us from jail?
Those who are free brain still in a cell
Locked in lies you taught to us
Then you mad cause we confused and don't give no...

11:40 AM CST
10-02-2015

The Next New Jim Crow

The new Jim Crow as articulated by Michelle
Shows how Black men are stuck in hell
Crimes white men get probation for
Black men get stuck behind a steel door

Bedrooms that double as bathrooms for drug crimes
People truly need rehabilitation not more time
Men with mental illness get arrested for sleeping
Death by officer because ain't no treatment

Too many locked up, ask a Koch brother
My dude doing 50—convicted coke brother
Both sides of the aisle say system untenable
They only true worry is appearing fiscally hospitable

I don't care why they want us free
My only worry is the real fee
The Information Age is skipping poor people
The next, new Jim Crow will have similar ripples

The new pariah will be an American hybrid
Poor felon that's uneducated—near dead
Locked in ghettos through GPS while drones watch
Can't leave your block—eternal block watch

They poisoned the food and water is tainted
Next, new Jim Crow turns us into aliens
Deformed bodies from bad milk and chicken
Highly processed, dumb minds made in a kitchen

You just watch how the game will evolve
The end result is control who you are
ISIL is destroying artifacts that prove Blackness
In bed with white civilization, do you see what's happening?

The fenna free poor people to kill ourself
Food, drugs, and cigarettes all contribute to ill health
We'll be free, fat and sick with no sense of culture
They want white domination, the method is being altered

9:55 AM
10-22-2015

Joshua Generation

The prolapse of morals
in the Black community
is not rapper's fault
blame those from 35 to 60

The mouth of preachers
runs with loquacity
sending us to slow death
following in sequacity

Too much insistence
on the fideistic
no understanding of Jesus
our lust is unrealistic

We need a resurgence
in our neighborhoods
no worries about designers
and always looking good

We must turn our dollars
into real wealth
no more handouts
do for self

Desire for white man's wealth
they stole from us
oxymoronic self of self
in Caucasian gods we trust

Those born after 1956
sent us down the drain
materialistic and agnostic
inability to use our brain

Only want to ride slick
desire for a white bitch
me too—no lies
because I'm sick

The hip hop generation
is just like Joshua
leaving old folks dead
taking what wasn't offered

12:05 PM CST
2-25-2016

Mental Complex

The guard tower is the white phallus
the dick in the Black man's ass
Inability to think of freedom
due to the watchful eyes of Mr. Charlie

Prisons are new plantations for slaves
new cotton is long sentences
Guards are new overseers
snitches still telling on Nat

Large companies profit from inmate labor
people on the street consumed in consumerism
Poor people are rural America's cows
no need for farms or widgets—just niggas

Panacea exist to rid us of the complex:
we must revolt with dollars
that will end white supremacy
Caucasian domination is predicated on mendacity

Black ignorance fuels the flames
we must buy books instead of purses
Brothers who are incarcerated
should go to rec and read non-fiction

The situation is precarious;
materialism leads to prison then death,
killing the spirit through your wallet—
Jesus can't save you if he is white

12:52 PM CST
11-21-2015

Who's/Whose Free?

Albert Woodfox is free
Black people still locked up
minds trapped in denial
spending borrowed dollars

To look good and be free
Black people are behind—
pockets, intellect, and neighborhoods
Mr. Charlie has you locked in

From Upper Marlboro to Southfield
to Stone Mountain niggas ain't free
riding slick, got a degree
desire to consume like a honkie

We need Potomac or Grosse Pointe money
Buckhead dollars for the hood
then the Americans from Africa
might be free

Until then Christ Jesus can't save us
because he's locked in solitary confinement
on 31st and Galena
help Jesus get free, so you can be

7:25 AM CST
2-20-2016

Prison Life Essay

L ife in prison is a daily struggle to muster a semblance of dignity, while not succumbing to virulent degradation, amid authoritarian captors whose manifest motive is to inflict debilitating and nefarious torture on its inhabitants. This process is concomitant with alternation of DNA to produce broken, servile people who become gluttons for the punishment. This condition is state-sanctioned, tacitly supported by the masses, and generally understood to be justified for committing crime.

The mornings start the day with a clarion call to breakfast and standing count. Even in a prison that flies an American flag, conditions are rife with injustice-filled cages and people blinded by the fog of humiliation, lack of visits, and threats of violence.

Sex is rampant in correctional institutions and provides a means for mental and physical relief as well as a tool for manipulation and bartering for goods and services. Some have sex with their celly, while other convicts look in the mirror of religion or recreation for solace and comfort.

Sitting in the chapel usually means being bombarded with messages of inadequacies for moral failure or perceived lack of fortitude. It's often overlooked that Paul spent a considerable amount of time in jail. Also, because of America's rampant, state-sponsored drug industry, narcotic K9s are as ubiquitous in prisons as they are in Florida traffic stops. Jesus is still alive in a prison in close proximity to all Americas.

The conundrum of the prison-industrial complex is it allows men to work for companies that wouldn't and doesn't hire then when not incarcerated. In less than the four minutes until count clears, an imbecile can figure who's working who from the four to six brands of merchandise available on canteen for purchase. The politicians and lobbyists are the hypocrites who tell lies of truth to a blind constituency that is unaware crime rates are down and tax dollars are going for an irremissible travesty of justice against the most vulnerable members of society.

Prison is a place of sordid debasement designed by master sadist. Tales of shower sex and quickies with fat COs are real. To stay alive one may have to make moves with thugs to circumvent the constant conflict between the System—represented by the guards—and the hate they mete out. Prisoners, like all humans, are appointed once to die. Some are men who die as heroic warriors like Dave Thomas and Danny Tanner; however, in jail, if you are weak, you will die myriad deaths.

It's the Morning

Day breaks over barbed-wire fences
Early sun competes with orange lights
Morning reflects her presence off concrete
How many more days until release?

Replete with grief; completed with sorrow
Tomorrow will start the same
Yesterday began with oatmeal and toast
Today there will be oatmeal and toast

When will my morning come?
I can't wait to hear my name
Until then I have to get up
Either for breakfast or count

The window doesn't let the sun in
Rays of light obscured by bars
Bars with light frame my existence
Days filled with yesterday's promises

8:03AM CST
9-03-2015

In a Prison that Flies an American Flag

In a prison that flies an American flag
Some men are locked down 23 hours

In a prison that flies an American flag
Brothers been in 15 years ain't got a GED

In a prison that flies an American flag
Guards selling shots of pussy for $50

In a prison that flies an American flag
White prisoners install fiber optic cables

In a prison that flies an American flag
Black convicts work in the kitchen

In a prison that flies an American flag
Inmates run to the gym and don't walk to the library

In a prison that flies an American flag
Mao Zedong is banned, but Hitler is read

In a prison that flies an American flag
They pay for men to get breasts and not degrees

In a prison that flies an American flag
Nineteen-year-olds suck off old men for shoes

In a prison that flies an American flag
Responsibility is taught without a vocation

In a prison that flies an American flag
Men have boyfriends yet conjugal visits are banned

In a prison that flies an American flag
Inmates look at Curves and won't read The Final Call

In a prison that flies an American flag
They know 2 Chains, but not Ta-Nehisi Coates

In a prison that flies an American flag
The stanzas for this piece were written

In a prison that flies an American flag
Representing the constant and consistent injustice

In a prison that flies an American flag
While propagating the tenets of white supremacy

In a prison that flies an American flag
Perpetuating the continued subjugation of the Aboriginal people
of the Earth

11:30 AM CST
10-18-2015

My Cage

I live in a bathroom
it doubles as a bedroom
When hungry it's a kitchen
sometimes it's my den

Writing letters it's an office
it's also a closet
A glorified storage space
for an adjudicated criminal

Relegated to my crimes
to time in a toilet
Sink water don't get hot
guards watch when I shit

I do have a window
in my caged hell
I see other zoo animals
walking around in aimless circles

12:51 PM CST
10-13-2015

The Fog

Rec yard bathed in fog
only the geese are free
guards locked in maze of denial
prisoners in labyrinth of confusion

The fog conceals the shame
geese fly away mocking me
guards hide behind authoritarianism
prisoners contribute to their own death

Pain shrouded by the fog
the geese understand
guards are locked in too
all prisoners choose their own prisons

7:29 AM CST
9-27-2015

No Visits

I ain't had a visit in five years
My mama scared of the highway
My BM got a baby by my brother
I had a girl, now she in Iowa dancing
I was reading the Bible
Now I go to Jumu'ah
Allah ain't make nobody come visit either

2:05 PM CST
9-22-2015

The Visit

Verisimilitude of care and affection
you sit across from me smiling
a smile full of bane guile
as you explicate that lie

Mind dancing with flagitious thoughts
you get up and get another soda
a soda worth the amount of your love
as you proclaim that lie

Calumny pours from your mouth
you grab my hand in a spurious gesture
a gesture that suggests I'm unaware of your hate
as you declare that lie

Spent the stash on him
you leave as they call my last name
a name we share, extirpated by fatuity
as you continue to live your truth—
with my money

2:37 PM CST
2-27-2016

My Celly

I hate sucking dick,
but I want him to do me
It make me feel like a fag
what if my boys see?

No one knows what we do,
but late at night we in bed
All over each other
fucking and giving head

It feel real good
I just hate doing it
It make me feel guilty
plus I'm a convict

Been in and out of jail
since stays in juvie
On the outs I'm with women
in the joint I get booty

I ain't gay at all—
just like what I like
Ain't no pussy in here
celly the bitch tonight!

12:32 PM CST
10-31-2015

Convict Mirror

Prison as far as my eye can see
Building after building made for you and me
You and me were meant to be free
Not in a eight by six with 13 inch TV

Toilet attached to the sink and wall
No more crimes, to any job I'll crawl
Mass housing for the poor called jail stalls
They crowd us in like it's a cattle call

Two thousand men in one joint, it's a small city
Fights over punks with real titties
Man lost an eye over the phone it's gritty
Not a sweet place, in fact real shitty

Lives lost to parole and truth in sentencing
My man on the Monfils case is clearly innocent
Want us imprisoned; we're not American citizens
Went from ghetto to barbed wire fence denizens

Locked me in—controlled niggas denizens
Poor, landless felon—obviously not a citizen
Black Savior of society, call me Pope Innocent
Judge never do us favors at sentencing

Pissed me off slapped him so hard drawers shitty
Dreams of a grisly murder consistently gritty
Did 20 years straight I miss my girl titties
Been in Wisconsin 30 years still reppin' the City

Only leave the unit when rec calls
No girls in jail so they fuck men in stalls
Begging the parole board on knees some crawl
So much time brothers go crazy and stare at walls

In prison they watch too much TV
No compromise my people must get free
Perfect example of what not to be—just look at me
Big Jimmie got family he rarely see

12:55 PM CST
2-28-2016

Sitting in Chapel (Sinner's Confession)

Burning desires with passion blazing
Conflagrant feelings inside my soul
Longing for you as he reads the Word
Heart filled with lust and not the Lord

You keep rubbing your arm against mine
Pressure of your leg makes concentration difficult
I want to rip the green khakis off
Let's make love on an alter of iniquity

Imprisoned in my body and this chair
Your ardor for me is palpable
Forget Jesus; let's go to your cell
I came to get right and my mind is wrong

The Lord is my Shepherd, but I'm horny
He'll separate the goats from the sheep
Lowly sinner damned to personal hell
Emotions in mental prison; body in prison

Fulfill my urges to baptize you in semen
Thoughts of lascivious abominations
I want to read every verse of your body
Wretched man interposed by licentiousness and redemption

11:38 AM CST
10-27-2015

Drug Dogs in Jail

Drug dog just searched my cell
Gestapo got me in concentration hell
I allowed the State to lock me in
selling drugs in jail ain't really a sin

My yard is like the projects
they selling weed, ass, and cigarettes
I'm in the drug treatment unit
heroin and suboxone constantly moving

German shepherd drinking out my bowl
I can't wait to take my ass home
The guards bring in most of the dope
search they ass; leave my cell alone

All the weed was smoked up yesterday
tobacco got chewed up Sunday
Right after church I met my guy
two bags of coffee for the stick I'll buy

No-knock raid in the penitentiary
don't scare me, I'm off 15th Street
Being getting searched since I was 12
nothing changed cause I'm in jail

White guards think it's funny
this is how the State make they money
Justify locking up poor, Black men
keep that nigga behind bars in the pen

My cell smell just like a dog
secretly taint my food with hog
The soy got men growing breasts
going home with vaginas is what's next

Most males locked up are pussy
lie about dicks they suck and dookie booty
Getting high to relieve the stress
or talk about who hoop the best

State and its victims' priorities are confused
DOC overfunded and prisoners need graduate school
Take the drug dogs to affluent senior highs
instead of worrying about the gram or two I sell just to get by

10:51 AM CST
2-23-2016

Conundrum

Prison as far
as my eye can see
Allowed devils to lock me in
these sadist have me

Poor choices
and lack of self-esteem
I wanted to smoke and fuck
wear $600 jeans

All day spent
at the bar
Shoulda became a lawyer
passed the bar

Now I'm locked in
it's count time
Just finished sweeping
literally made two dimes

From $30 an hour
to less than 30 cents
Allowed the State to fuck me
now I fuck other men

I don't have much,
but my balls and my words
The State is draining me
I cry through expletives and verbs

7:48 AM CST
2-16-2016

Four Minutes until Count Clears

Dark, cold Wisconsin morning
Count was late clearing and I was hard
Hard and horny ready for a quickie—no moaning
We must be silent, last time they heard you on the yard

The heightening crescendo of our bodies was harmony
Was it me on top of you or you on top of me?
Who cares, our magic flip flops fill you with thoughts of me
Strong smells: sweat, passion, lust—oh to be free

Unchain me from this sentence if just for three minutes
Bodies pressed close as sweat falls and tension builds
Not finished, but you thank me; my dick probes your mouth like
a dentist
I put it back in you, we continue, my mind fills with azalea fields

Calm, tranquil place you take me to; relaxed yet tense
An oxymoronic sense of fear and comfort
I push in deeper; you say, "Further...," I see the fence
Out the window and the freeway you should dump her

Your wife don't know you like getting fucked, love getting
fucked!
I'm almost free; I see cars on the Interstate
I want to cum so bad—wildly your hips bucked
Just about home, I bust, I couldn't wait

8:37 AM CST
6-22-2015

Who's Working Who?

Police bring in weed and cigarettes
They selling pussy too—who's next?
You can buy head and ass too
Men and women guards all screw

The prison is an open market
Right price is the target
People hustling to stay high
Others to get by

Young men sell they self for a TV
Old men wash clothes for canteen
Guards work doubles for they habits
Nurse call you to HSU to secretly grab it

All staff and convicts work a show
Get over quick so they can go
On to the next mark to get over
When the State rolled 'um both in short order

5:15 PM CST
10-11-2015

Canteen Day

Everybody making nachos
pay me my money
Skipping tonight's hotdogs
if he short it won't be funny

My man moved to Q Building
I took over his store
Lames don't wanna pay
just drop it at my door

The punk owed 50—
checked out to the box
Old Man James owe 30
on the outs I sold him rocks

In here I got a sucka store
2 for 1 or 1 and a half
Run up a bill you can't pay
that's yo ass

Put the flops on Dre
about my doe
Doubled White Phil bill
he was late going to the store

About four checked out
didn't have my merch
I will catch you
down at rec or up at church

You will bring my chili
those meats you owe
I need that cheese
thanks for stopping at the Inmate Store

12:17 PM CST
3-01-2016

Hypocrite

Two grown ass niggas laying in the bed
You ain't in for life, why you giving head?
Released in four months, what is you on?
You got a son, daughter, and wife at home

Been to the joint about six or seven times
Now I'm wondering why you do crimes
I think you get locked up just to screw
You don't get money on the streets, so what do you do?

You always asking about who a fag
Can't wait for the punks to get off the bus in drag
You the first one there, canteen bag in hand
Constantly gump stalking—jail Candyman

You enjoy boy pussy when you locked up
We all know sometime you get fucked
Been doing boys doggystyle since juvie
At supermaxs and minimums you want dookie booty

Nothing wrong with having your fun
It's that you a hypocrite and the main one
Always laughing and joking when it's really you
Performing fellatio and swallowing cum too

5:25 PM CST
10-08-2015

Lies of Truth

The chick I'm writing is 47
I'm 30
She wants to be my mama
Take care of me

I write her nasty letters
Tales of sweaty sex
She sent me a TV
Pay my mama rent next

I'm kinda wrong
She on SSI
Cashing in food stamps
So I can get by

I feed her lies
She send me money
Talk of marriage
I call her honey

She bring my mama
And my kids
Up on visits
So I continue to fib

WRITTEN IN BLOOD   55

When I get out
I may move in
Keep taking her bread
What a sin

I don't feel bad
Prison is hard
She help me out
I'll keep up the canard

5:40 PM CST
2-04-2016

Shower Sex

Relentless pound game I put on your ass
Fat, white ass make me cum fast
Your wife don't know you take dick so well
Hole between your cheeks is the direct route to hell

We fucked in the shower 12:40 late night
No one was really up, your ass so tight
I used conditioner to lube up the hole
You grab your ankles and the anus unfolds

You moan out, "Daddy...," but I think your trash
When I'm not in you, Black people you bash
In and out, my joint demands retribution
You relish the punishment and cum profusely

I quickly pull out; push you to your knees
You suck off the conditioner and your own shit with ease
I bust in your mouth, the rest on your face
If the wife don't send no more money, that's the last taste

8:32 PM CST
8-20-2015

Quickie with a Fat CO Bitch

Damn it's wet
I ain't had no pussy in three years

She fat as hell, but it don't stink
I wouldn't have cared, that's the least of my fears

I'm fenna bust
I need that phone and them squares tomorrow

That nutt felt good
Next time I'll make her swallow

12:15 PM CST
6-12-2015

Make Moves with Thugs

I got a big dick, I won't lie
you know Sgt. Foster, I nutted on her thigh
I usually prefer if she swallow—no evidence
plus I enjoy her deep throat—Ms. Decadence

She do whatever for me that I ask
money to my BM and I fuck her in the ass
she bring in cell phones, squares, and cush
brought me in a pair of J's to complete my look

I'm DMX and these niggas from Nebraska
they done got a heart condition about the size of Canada
police keep checking my cell and holding receipts
they ain't found nothing, but I'm still losing sleep

I'm getting about a stack a week from dro alone
I sell one cell that keep my girl lights on
the suboxone move fast and the money just right
I even put a few Gs away for a stormy night

I'm about to go slow, have her work with the Kings
Baldhead Carlos and nem can move the loosies and the lean
it worked well until CO Doogan started talking
sick since I started fucking because he been stalking

He told on me, Carlos, the Natives, and the Asians
we all was fucking, getting plugged, and receiving payments
whole operation knocked we was shipped to max
couldn't fire Foster she took disability for her back

BM back selling pussy, really don't think she stopped
Doogan got whooped, put in the hospital, now he a cop
I did a 360 in the box and they charged me too
beat the case, but the little money put up is through

I had a good run, don't feel too bad
sent some bread home, that made me feel glad
this new joint alright and I see a new victim:
fat, divorced, no self-esteem—hello CO Hickman

2:45 PM CST
9-01-2015

You and I: Convict Guard Hate

Told me to hurry up, ole' bitch ass police
Heard you the first time should put you to sleep
You fake as that watch hanging from your wrist
Your wife is fucking Captain Smith, she a cheating-fake bitch

I know your wife is a hoe
She made sergeant and you still a CO
Got your daughter a job here wit' her fat, lazy ass
Saw you nephew, the queer, switch down the tier fast

Done told me three times to finish my food
Should bust you in yo' shit for disturbing my mood
I quit taking my meds about two months ago
I might pick you up and stomp you into the floor

Say one more thing that blue shirt gone be red
Already got a concurrent five for hitting a guard in the head
You read the record why I'm at this max
I batter police, broke CO Jones back

You can call chow, but I'm still eating
I got 20 minutes, do what you do, but I ain't leaving
You trying to look tough and come my way
I keep chewing, taking my time, then you yell, "Hey!"

You get loud, "Boy I told you chow time is threw!"
I get up, call you a fag, and say, "Fuck you!"
You look scared, but hesitantly talk shit
I tell you bust a move, let's dance pale ole' bitch

You hit the panic button, didn't know what to do
I know yo' heart pump piss and you hide behind blue
You move toward me when the goon squad come in
I figure I'll hit you anyway cause I know how it end

You on the ground as I choke you breathless
I get hit from behind, my balls kicked—reckless
You in the corner on all fours near death
I laugh cause I don't give no fuck about that

You know not to fuck wit' me no mo
I tried to crush your larynx, bring your esophagus through yo jaw
You get FMLA and I catch a new charge
I don't care cause smashing honkies is my job

White crackers been beating on niggas for 500 years
I'll even the score and separate you from yo kids
You say no remorse, lock 'um up, see what he did
I say look what you did to me, you deserved it you pig

5:28 PM CST
6-11-2015

Appointed Once to Die

Next cell over the man died
Right on the toilet—pants down
May have killed himself
Or worried himself to death

Scared me so much I didn't care
People acting concerned but wasn't
They was thinking about they own mortality
Everybody got a number

In prison, everybody wants to get out
Guards want to go to the bar
Convicts want to go home
Lifers want to go to heaven

Death ain't scary when you seen him
He is just doing his job
Sometimes it's hard to avoid him
Hopefully, he'll stop playing with me

12:11 PM CST
11-17-2015

Heroic Warrior (Ode to Tanner)

Loved by the real
Child of the Great Spirit
Gone too soon

It's only been
a few hours
and it feels like years

True Chief
Man of the people
Heart of gold

Some of us are crying
our hearts are broken
we know you are home

Full of life
Wisdom seeker
Leader of men

Our love can't
die because it's
eternal—like you

Humble soul
Gifted mind
Artistic creativity

Why are you gone?
Part of me has
died with you

Noble servant
Wonderful father
Good son
Heroic warrior

9:04 PM CST
5-06-2016

Ontology/Psychology/Spirituality Essay

The blood is being sucked out of the psyche of poor people, through spiritual and economic warfare, performed by preacher pimps who utilize the pulpit as a get-rich-quick scheme. Marginalized people that have no ontological sense of self are able to be by psychologically controlled through religious practices that are not alive in the Spirit.

He who made me and you is demanding retribution for the enslavement of Africans in the Americas. Chattel slavery is over and poor people are still being enslaved because pastors tell them to pray and forgive—people who hate them—instead of revolt with dollars and rebuild their community like Nehemiah. The progression of ascendant degradation from knowing God, and walking in Sonship, to being reduced to materialistic slaves and strippers, who survive on hope and prayers, is the framework of Americanized Christianity and watered-down Islam. Forgotten people are left, by their government, religious leaders, and community activists, alone to be depressed in thoughts of death.

American churches take in billions of dollars every year. Why do we have profound poverty in communities where there is a church on every corner? Prisoners in these impoverished areas are locked in thoughts of moral depravity, which is partially a result of economic injustice, and a yoke of blues Billie couldn't even conjure.

I have had, and enjoy, sex with women and men. I don't believe I was born bisexual; however, because of being molested, by two older cousins, I am truthfully lost and hurt. I would rather pick one sexuality or have someone pick me. My personal belief is that most people aren't born gay or bisexual; and, due to circumstances—molestation, imprisonment, lack of resources, substance abuse disorders, etc.—people will do what feels good and/or gets them what they want or need. For the most part, the church demonizes non-heterosexual people when there are a considerable number of LGBTQ and people who have sex with the same sex, and don't self-identify as gay, in the pews and that exclusion and relegation is the true sin.

The temple will be destroyed because we are gods—all of us— and we are not fulfilling the mandate of the Most High. A Black man's faith built the ancient world and his back built the New World. It doesn't even matter if you are bipolar, suffer from substance abuse, lack shelter, or need food; the church should provide those services and more. How can there be a God, whom you claim to serve, when your brothers and sisters are denied basic necessities?

Preacher Pimps

Preacher pimps multiply sins through greed
Gimme 10%, I'll give you what you need
If you just have faith like a mustard seed
Gimme 10%, I'll give you what you need

Sister Jones was sick, almost dead, on Tuesday
I blessed her with oil, she was healed Saturday
Came to sunrise service to give me my 10% Sunday
Maybe she wasn't healed cause she died on Monday

I need a new Ferrari so I can look blessed
My testimony is I used to pimp hoes, I must confess
Now I feed the flock and should look my best
Come on church, empty your pockets you know the rest

It's a stick up robbery, I want ten talents
Your kids don't need college funds, but check my balance
The building fund is low so open your purse
Plus 10% for me, please give until it hurts

I ain't straining gnats, I'm no Pharisee
I'm the epitome of Christian leadership straight from 2 Timothy
Nah, you about as bad as Balaam, a crooked soothsayer
If we was listening to jazz you'd be a smooth operator

Took the widows two mites and the crippled man's mat
Leaving the people hungry, what kind of preacher is that?
You aren't building industry to give your parishioners jobs
You take from the community and play with God

Let's be like Jesus and start acting Jewish
Own banks and stores, not spending money like we foolish
Maybe close one church and merge with the next
Use the other building as a business and start to collect

Get our dough up instead of to the pastor
If he was really like Paul he'd be a tent master
Providing for self and definitely not taking from me
But showing true religion by rebuilding our community

4:42 PM CST
9-02-2015

Are You Alive in the Spirit?

Praise God, lift up the serpent—Jesus
Who is God? We knew Her in Africa
The enemy tried to fool you, now you can't please us
Who you ask? Your cousins in the Diaspora

Your first mother was Isis, your father is Set
A holy union with a baby boy who came
Jesus—you celebrate spend Xmas dollars to go in debt
You've forgotten Osiris the first Christ name

His daddy killed him, original Black violence
Osiris is dead, but mama brought him back
Fanned life in the royal penis, death won't be silenced
Here comes Moses, I mean Horus another true Black

Osarsiph was his name; we have historical evidence
An apostate priest of Ra, the one true God
Yah fell into disrepute; they left guided by Providence
Them people was Black and the Reed Sea was a bog

They got free, then got mad, back to slavery
Bondage to golden calves sounds familiar to me
Big rims and Coach bags—the African-American enemy
Mixing Els and Truth was the new decree

Jesus—ain't dead he's up in Waupun
Brought to the Promised Land on the ship Liberty
Twenty million died on the trip across the pond
Gave me a new name now for religion I pay a fee

Preacher pimps still ride chariot I mean Rolls Royce
Large white pyramids filled with black ghosts
Malachi says you must pay me—your tithe—no choice
Can I hold a Black Love rally at your church—sorry won't host

The original Temple was political and economic
A psychological center with healthy outcomes
They produced real gods, not a weak trick
Return to real Christianity don't act so dumb

Do you represent Nigeria and Kente clothe
Or France, Italy, and Jimmy Choo
Your religion and your money are linked don't be a sloth
I want you to study whose progeny are you

You scream stop snitching, but go tell it on Facebook
How the white man takes your dollars and you're proud
Bought the kids $300 jeans, he got you, legal crook
Clicked "Like" to die to be in the "in" crowd

Pastor lied to you; put 10% in an IRA
Boycott business that don't support your people
I don't preach politics from the pulpit they say
They should or they risk pulling you to a hell depot

Pre-colonial Black Africa had him—Jesus
Only white man we met in America was Uncle Sam
In God we trust is on a dollar, they fucked us
Enslaved us to fossilized customs now we worship the damned

Unknown time
Unknown date

He Who Made Me

I'm coming out this closet I'm in
Sorry, no fags or dykes at church—it's a sin
What about those who live at the casino?
Well, Mother Jones tithes when she hits at bingo

I'm coming out this Sunday, I don't care
Not in this sanctuary, people may stare
You got dope fiends, liars and rapist too
I know, but the LGBT community can't come through

We are God-fearing people, filled with the Ghost
It seems you all are hypocritical the most
You're worried about who I sleep with and love
When Jesus preached righteousness from up above

The Word says for me to work out my salvation
You church folks won't pick my final destination
I am created in the image of God Almighty
I don't need the church's approval to be who He made me

11:35 AM CST
9-13-2015

Stripper's Prayer

Lord, be with me
as I work this pole
and as old perverts
touch my asshole

Lord, I need
your help tonight
I have to watch the hoes
and the customers not right

Keisha keep stealing
some of my tips
one more time
and I'm busting her lip

Sparkle always want
to wear my shoes
I was being nice,
but I'm fenna get rude

I popped two pills
and smoked a blunt
please keep me safe
as fake ballers front

I'm just trying
to make rent money
new shoes for my son
this shit ain't funny

This lame ass nigga
keep screaming pimping
can't knock a real hoe
my money I'm not giving

God, you made me
into a renegade
I work poles and do shows
to try to get paid

8:04 PM CST
3-04-2016

Progression of Ascendant Degradation

G-Ma raised me
my mama was on crack—still
is on crack
turning tricks in our basement
Is that my daddy?

G-Ma cooked greens and
black-eyed peas
my mama boiled hot dogs

G-Ma started to go to bingo—a lot
I had to pick up the pieces
sometimes the rent was late
or my sister needed tampons

It was mandatory that I hustle
I would let old men fuck me
for money in our basement
Then I picked up a pack
I'm the man now

This cell ain't so bad—
and they serve hot dogs
Is that my daddy?

I need some canteen
I might let a old man
fuck me in the bathroom
Do this cell hall have a basement?

8:29 AM CST
2-05-2016

Alone

She walks alone
his eyes dilated
he rapes her
leaves her violated

His mama cries
at the trial
her only son
she's in denial

Her boyfriend molested
her young son
penetrated him nightly
filled with cum

She was smoking
her son confused
mad at himself
quit middle school

Secretly raping girls
birth of domination
real live predator
scared and alienated

Followed this woman
for two days
waiting for time
to separate legs

Beat her mercilessly
raped her twice
killed her soul
alone that night

6:02PM CST
2-24-2016

Depressed in Thoughts of Death

lethargy in life
tired of the tumult
ready to die

land of the living is lost
sleep seems sensuous
soul never to be found

angel of death
please come to me
thoughts of utter morbidity

11:36 AM CST
11-05-2015

Prisoner's Thoughts

I tell myself lies
so I don't lose hope
I pray to God
mama ain't back on dope

Can't wait to get out
play with my kids
Until now I'm cell-bound
doing time for what I did

Daddy still drinking
my kids missing class
BM at the casino
my brother off cash

Kept moving packs
spent all the money
Lawyer took the rest
stomach feeling funny

Grandma just died
my uncle is sick
Auntie on dialysis
my niece turning tricks

Family falling apart
I can't even help
Stuck in jail
can't even help myself

12:50 PM CST
12-01-2015

Prison Blues

life winnows between yesterday's dust
vapid existence, bereft of joy
bars confirm an inactivity in listlessness
languid thoughts so obsequious

tired of living; scared of suicide
demise written in judgment of conviction
propensity of proclivities found me guilty
inclination of desolation imprisons my soul

replete with ambiguous indifference
future of torture designed for masochists
sustenance unfit for consumption
backed against walls of potential

sleepy from provisional reality
surrounded by ambulating dead bodies
masticating souls surfeit on lies
populations perish in penitentiaries

2:51 PM CST
9-04-2015

Bisexual

I wanna eat some pussy
maybe suck a dick
Wouldn't mind getting fucked in the ass
and I wanna fuck that bitch

Two women or a wife and husband
three college guys cum dumping
I don't care, let's have sex
her, we, him, or whoever's next

I enjoy a real hard cock
I also like when balls knock
on my ass or me pounding pussy
I have fun and don't bust fast

11:28 AM CST
9-15-2015

Truthfully Lost and Hurt

I wasn't born gay
some people are
older cousin used to suck my dick—how sick
early experiences sometime stick

To me an asshole or
vagina feel similar
A mouth is a mouth
I stopped counting partners

I took an HIV test
got vaccinated against Hep A & B
I've always loved myself
not always my behavior

I know who I am
I'm also aware of presentation
My heart longs for companionship—
please, somebody, want me

7:50 AM CST
9-27-2015

The Temple Will Be Destroyed

Jesus is still being lynched
in American courtrooms
on the streets of Staten Island
paddy wagons in Baltimore

Tamar is still being raped
in American homes
on the bed's of brothers
apartments that lack protection

Judas is still cheating
in American boardrooms
in office parks of Sunnyvale
incubators in Austin

Rahab is still selling pussy
in American alleys
on the internet in Milwaukee
brothels outside of Vegas

Time is still being repeated
America is the Promised Land
Truth is not mocked;
You always reap what you sow
The Temple will be destroyed

unknown time
unknown date

Black Man's Faith

Forlorn hope, my soul is empty
Void of life; a cocoon of nothingness
Dejected spirit, so lost, forgotten by God
Existence reminiscent of death on the cross

Bereft of the pleasures of living
Utterly consumed by the vicissitudes of circumstance
Thoughts of death dance joyfully in my head
Coffins seem safe, quiet, and free

Desolate understanding filled with grief
Wretched ruminations provide momentary solace
Cries from my psyche echo in the dark
Discomfort unable to be assuaged only exacerbated

No amelioration for the pain of my sorrow
Memories of happiness buried under caustic hurt
Tears pollinate burdens that proliferate exponentially
I can't fathom the possibility of being healed or whole

unknown time
unknown date

Bipolar 1 with Non-Mood Congruent Psychotic Features

I've been sleep for three days
Palled from my lack of energy
I just want to sleep
I'm in one of my moods

Pondering death because I'm scared of life
Wearisome from my vapid existence
I wish these voices would shut up
Be quiet!

I wonder what it's like to be free
Free from incessant slumber
Free of medication that dries my mouth
Free from voices working to kill me

What is that sound?
Cogitating on pills, a gun, or hanging
It's been two months and I'm back on meds
Better get up, a check's in the mail

Transported to Macy's and Harbor House
Spent two stacks real fast
Ecstatic from euphoric-filled shopping
Shut up, I'm not killing myself today

I'm down to my last Ben frank
Get a 50 sack, some roll-ups, and beer
No meds for me—I feel good!
Maybe I'll go get a payday advance

My cycle is endless
Sometimes it's drugs or I shop or go have sex
Then I crash and, occasionally, burn
with chlamydia, debt or a deviated septum

Only thing keep me right is Jesus and meds
Most times he don't even care
I cloyingly accept my issues
Shut up! Leave me alone!

12:38 PM CST
9-29-2015

It Doesn't Even Matter

Thugs in dresses
the world has changed
men wearing panties
they ain't even gay

Sexuality is fluid
be who you want
you like men and women
no need to front

Straight, gay, or bisexual
it doesn't even matter
be your true self
others opinions are just chatter

You were created perfectly
God doesn't make garbage
you are one with I AM
walk in that knowledge

12:25 PM CST
12-01-2015

How Can There Be a God?

The man sat on a bench made of wood
and said there is no God
under a sun that illuminated his surroundings
and said there is no God
he asked about our girls in Nigeria
and said there is no God
wondered about a three-year-old being raped
and said there is no God
is doing a life bid, with parole
and said there is no God
eats at least 21 meals a week
and said there is no God
changes clothes everyday
and said there is no God
I asked him, "What if God is inside of you?"
He felt God doesn't provide answers.
I attempted to explain and, then, I gave up. A sage
once told me not to argue with a stop sign.

2:40 PM CST
9-21-2015

Love Essay

Love is founded in Truth and Righteousness or it resembles love and is a similitude of lust, idolatry, and confusion. A resurgence is needed that ushers in a Black Love Empire that allows us to love ourselves, our children—Kayla and Junior and Shaunte and Deshawn—all of them, and, by purposeful action, our communities.

My heart cries when I witness the lack and misuses of love semblances. A mouse exhibits more love for its offspring and surroundings than some humans display. I am a victim and a perpetrator of love tenets and often think I'm in love. I have surreptitiously and overtly tried to manipulate romantic situations that then become forbidden love.

During a portion of my incarceration, my love belonged to another and I was filled with thoughts of JD and DJ. Things didn't work as I hoped and I experienced rejected love with my dumb ass! The circumstances surrounding the relationship were seriously funny because I has hurt, yet whole, and definitely stronger and wiser as a result of the experience. It was not as innocent as my first love—Sheila; however, it was replete with similar passion and intrigue.

Usually, relationships have three sides: his argument, her response, and a synthesis. All love isn't that clear cut and sometimes it's his response to a new relationship with you and

Nikki. The prologue to an affair usually comes before the affected partner becomes aware and is left begging the other, "please don't leave."

In order for us and the kids to have a viable future, we must cultivate a love predicated on reality. The truth of love shines bright for our kids when we teach responsibility through spirituality, truth in actions, and love as a lifestyle.

Love Is

Love is an action,
predicated on self-preservation,
manifested through positive living
and healthy choices

Love is an ability,
based on protection,
shown by utilizing wisdom
and making sound decisions

Love is spiritual,
affirmed on Truth,
proven by activating righteousness
and reflecting I AM

Sex, murder, hate, lies,
theft, and confusion can be
evidence of love; however,
they should never be confused with
Love

12:46 PM CST
3-24-2016

Black Love Empire

Running around here watching Empire and El Chapo
while the white man cuts off your balls with gusto
Building civilizations based on white supremacy
and divorcing you from your hard-earned currency

Your empire should be built on Black Love
with big hugs for ancestors who never peddled drugs
and opened stores without calling women whores
    or bitches;
no dreams of a pale girl with white man's riches

Your shouts down the alley shouldn't be
"Ah, nigga, what you got for me?"
They should be, "Black Power!"
yet you rush to tell me that died in 1973

Barak got elected and we's free
to happily date Ms. Daisy
Too many on displays in the penitentiary
while our kids languish in poverty

It's 2,000 billionaires; only ten Black
you desire integration and don't want to go back
Go back to Africa for what? I'm from Chicago,
it's dirty and they got AIDS in the Congo

Everybody wasn't kings and queens, but we had respect
taught the white man to walk upright and stand erect
Our mothers birthed the universe and midnight sky
mama was the sacrificial savior—died for you and I

The four blood mysteries made her God
we worshiped at her feet now she's just a façade
Contacts and blonde hair; fake ass and breasts
Nikki and Kim in a blender—hot ghetto mess

Our fathers were men, not d-boy decoys
we had slavery too, but it wasn't a scam or a ploy
They were captured and became a part of us
we didn't separate families to the back of the bus

Prior to the Atlantic slave trade we had it made
universities and paved streets while they were in caves
Then life imploded and human trafficking exploded
one chief mad at that king, all the people became exploited

Remember who you are and where you come from
you weren't created to shake up heroin, selling pills to bums
Supposed to set the world on fire
cut dreams of being Barksdale from *The Wire*

Provide abundantly for them five kids you made
instead of being mad at they mama for that $40 you gave
Which wasn't enough and you blame her
for selling some pussy cause you ain't come through sir

She did what she had to do to make it happen
life is desolate, improvised, and sex is a weapon
It shouldn't be if you was building a Black Empire
you'd rather get knocked and become the town crier

To combat the feelings of shame and sting of poverty
she gave ya guy some because she was hungry, not horny
Then you call her a hoe for busting a few moves
when you weren't able to make it do what it do

So remember you do have a plethora of options
lawyer, doctor, engineer, not just street pharmacist
Live a life worthy of living—stand tall, be proud
and demand for you and your community Black Love now!

unknown time
9-08-2015

Kayla and Junior

Alone with four, pale yellow walls
My daughter gives me a kiss
I'm hallucinating—I'm alone
Her mama moved to Nashville
She still gone be her there
My mama ain't seen my son in two years
Are these walls yellow or off-white?
Am I alone with my mind or myself?
I only have pictures of my daughter

2:25 PM CST
9-22-2015

Mouse

Beautiful man with caramel skin
Round, fat ass I want to get in
Soft black hair reflects the sun
Desire to blow you makes me cum

You look like a god: noble and stately
My wish is to lay with you, us both naked
I'd stop writing if you were my man
Forgo my life to live out your plans

I want you deep inside of my soul
Passion unleashed; fantasies unfold
Visions of you run through my mind
Two sweaty prisoners making love sublime

I see your dick through your sweats
I hear you like old men, but I want you next
On the rec yard and at the gym
I make reasons to talk and see you again

These are all just thoughts in my head
Don't even know if you want me in bed
We rarely talk and like different things
I'm cosmopolitan and you have simple dreams

I want my life to include yours
Walks on the beach, making love on the shore
Spend every day looking deep into your eyes
And every night between your thighs

8:50 PM CST
10-12-2015

My Heart Cries

My kids are in need of a father
I am in need of wisdom
My daughter calls her boyfriend Daddy
I want to buy her shoes for school
My son is in foster care
If I wasn't in jail he would be at home
My children were forced to be adults
I allowed the State to care for me
My heart cries in my cell at night
I flip the wet pillow over
My kids are in need of a father
I am in need of wisdom
My daughter boyfriend sell heroin
I fear she may end up like her mother
My son is a thief and a liar
I hope he does not end up like his father
My father never knew his father
I never really knew mine
My heart cries in my cell at night
I flip the wet pillow over

2:37 PM CST
9-25-2015

I Think I'm in Love with You

Touching you brings new excitement
Your presence fulfills my joy
This new love is playful
My feelings are serious and sincere

I think I am in love with you
I know I am in love with you
Apprehensive of consequences
Allowing myself to feel—again

I feel the happiness in your smile
My shirt smelled like you
Your soft hands incite pleasure
Your eyes tell your truth

I don't know how long
My wish is forever
Nothing lasts that long
Let's make every day special

8:04 AM CST
11-11-2015

Surreptitiously

Stealing furtive glances
When I see you at chow
Secret passion unknown
I want you right now

To be inside of you
In your safe place
Away from steel doors
Moving at a lover's pace

How can we do it?
Conceal this secret
My heart is yours
You must keep it

Can we love here?
In these cages
What will we do?
Feelings in deep stages

5:04 PM CST
11-01-2015

Forbidden Love

Ascendant sentiments unable to be dissipated
Indomitable feelings formed in secret
Rectitude is impugned in favor of felicity
Proscribed effusions actuated surreptitiously

Heart manacled due to deprecation of society
Other inmate's solecism causes you consternation
Perforce, due to circumstances, you fear ignominy
Your soul is ineffaceable and they already know

Allow me to succor your shame
Turn your dread to sublime delectation
The heights of our love are insuperable
Your smile brings suffusions of halcyon

Enamored by the innocence of your affection
Secret kisses presage passionate nights
All clandestinity will end when we share a cell
Solicitous feelings replaced with animalistic excitement

Two lost souls inexorably linked
I am your preceptor of true love
Thorough in pedantry of the recondite language
You are my paramour—forever more

10-30-2015
12:16 PM CST

JD and DJ

Black and white skin contrasted like piano keys
Ass on my face, my tongue licks your hole and you're pleased
Round beautiful cheeks I squeeze as I rim the circle
Tongue fucking you fast while daddy's dick you gargle

You moan in pleasure and deep throat my piece
I got you so wet your boy pussy is in heat
You beg me to fuck you; I keep eating you out
Both moaning and thrusting, we'll climax no doubt

You stop sucking, jump off, and get on all fours
Doggystyle time—this fat, white ass I explore
No need for lube, it's ready and dripping
You sphincter relaxed on the dick enjoying the feeling

Whimpers of ecstasy indicate I'm doing good
Killing this white, ghetto booty straight from the hood
Ghetto white boy loving the Black cock
I wanna bust, but you beg, "Don't stop!"

I pull out, you lay on the bed spread eagle
I say taste your ass, you quickly suck it so eager
I return the nasty favor—lick and probe that flower
You grab my head, push my face in, "Deeper," you holler

I'm pounding this hole, you lay there and take it
I'm gripping this ass, your body is shaking
You call me Daddy, grab me close and we kiss
Your eyes roll back; it's obvious you love my dick

Not touching yourself, but you ass and cock are cumming
I start busting my nutt and ass juice is flowing
I'm still stroking hard getting everything out
You look happy, that OH face covers your mouth

I'm very content, but now I got weird feelings
We just supposed to be fucking not having heart dealings
I ask, "Are we together, can I call you mine?"
You say, "I still got the BM, but it's me and you
plus I fuck next time."

1:32 PM CST
8-29-2015

My Dumb Ass

Crying as I write this
I feel you slipping away
You never were there
So you can't stay

What can I do?
I want you happy
Can I make that happen?
One of us play Daddy

I'm torn and frustrated
Heart wrenched in the tumult
Confused and torn
Reaching for the unknown

Do you want me to bow?
Play the submissive role
Be who you tell me
Do as I'm told

I know I'm not young
No brown hair or baby fat
I never was her
You do know that?

Maybe I took seriously
Your passing desires
I wanted a friend
To be set on fire

I don't know you
I wish I did
Holding on to the fake
I'm grown, but acting like a kid

9:10 AM CST
1-03-2016

Rejected Love

Heartbroken and confounded
Desire to cry muffled by grief
Longing for love to feel whole
Past faults scare emotions away

I want you to have all of me
You seem to want nothing:
My body, my mind, my canteen
I will give you everything

You won't even talk to me
My reputation must embarrass you
You introduced yourself to me
I wasn't looking for you

You asked to be penetrated
My manhood is your muse
I compromised my mental fortitude
Lost inside myself, by myself

7:30 AM CST
9-21-2015

Seriously Funny Thoughts
(Musings on Sex and Race)

I prefer Black women
I fuck white men
I'll play a white girl
A threesome with friends

I rarely fuck Black men
We been through enough
It's hard being African-American
Who needs a dick in the butt?

White boys seem to love it—
Cock in the mouth
Gimme a Native or Hispanic
I'll turn his ass out

I really want a wife—
A bisexual beauty
For foursomes with couples
Nasty sex—real gooey

This is fun, but serious
I can't be a racist
I'm a poor, Black felon
I don't run the nation

An articulation of feelings
Why I fuck white boys
Especially the wiggers
It's fun like a toy

I haven't been honest
There's a white boy I loved
I really have a heart
Obviously, I'm no thug

5:37PM CST
date unknown

Sheila

The chance meeting on the bus
Due to an old, new friend
On our way to different schools
First love I ever knew

My dad would drop me off
Or I would catch the bus over
I can still smell your perfume
And remember your room on the right

You were as beautiful as your mother
I didn't like her boyfriend
We didn't date enough
I was actually very afraid

You were my dream girl locked away
My mother said I wanted white girls,
But you are Black and Mexican?!
I found your light skin problematic

Always trying to please my mama
I ended up injuring my soul
Should have acted like I felt
Loved you until we were old

Our first time was magically awkward
Your mom bought us condoms and lube
Started heavy petting on the sofa
Ended up naked in your room

Young lovers filled with confusion
Our relationship didn't last
Should have taken you to the prom
Too bad for me—we know how it ends

12:50 PM CST
10-28-2015

His Argument

I break up with the mama and the kids
stop paying rent where they all live
Take the electric and the cable out my name
go to my old BM house with no shame

Her new son call me Daddy anyway
not really mad at the kids, it's the games she play
Supposed to be home and phone ringing
right to voicemail and I'm steaming

She told me she was at the mall
my guy seen her on 76th Street with Big Paul
Because she creeping and humping
the kids and the bills will be suffering

It's like be up front and tell me
we used to have threesomes back in 2003
I don't care who you screw or what you do
What I ask is that you not play me for a fool

4:35 PM CST
11-29-2015

Her Response

Me and Big Paul is not having sex
we making moves, busting fake checks
The PO was on you to get a job
I went back to grinding it out with the mob

Paul and my brother grew up together
if I was cheating you wouldn't know better
Cut off my electric and cable if you want
back on—same day—you know I don't front

Them threesomes is old and I don't like coochie
I did enjoy when you and Nate banged me in the booty
You know I'm a freak, but why would I cheat?
We been together for years, you know I don't creep

Truth is I didn't want to bruise your ego
when you was locked up I sold pills and diesel
Me and my kids will never be homeless
don't no man make me and you know this!

4:46 PM CST
11-29-2015

Argument, Response, Synthesis

The problem with Black relationships
is the lack of love among participants
Two people together isn't physical, it's spiritual
grow together and soar like an eagle

We lack marriage and home ownership
yet we buy a lot of purses and go on trips
Vacations are fun after you buy a house
instead we give enemies our money and run our mouth

We argue, fight, and kill over designer brands
it would be nice to die for our own land
In order for Black people to be respected
we must use our money and mind as a weapon

Begin to love yourself first and family
save money, don't spend, kick Arabs out our community
Buy up blocks and get rid of preacher pimps
go to college, open businesses and be strong Black citizens

5:00PM CST
11-29-2015

You and Nikki

Time ain't on my side
and I got a whole load
My girl said she'd ride,
but she left for Nicole

My kids got two mamas
I'm stuck in a cell
I left her this my karma
payback is hell

Love we shared is priceless
my heart broken and shattered
Tears fall in silence
I thought what we had mattered

You and Nikki be happy
I wish you both well
Didn't mean to get sappy
just hate I'm in jail

12:10 PM CST
10-08-2015

Prologue (You and Nikki)

My girl left me for my baby mama
it was unbelievable heart trauma
We planned a threesome—no strings
BM on my face, wifey on her knees

I get knocked with 50 grams of brown
facing 15, lawyer got it knocked down
I still got eight and it cost 30K
son mother and my girl start moving yay

BM shake the boy, but wifey know girl—
got fronted a slab by Old Man Earl
Grinding at the spot feelings grew
no longer three, now it's just two

They getting money and sucking monkey
I'm stuck behind walls like a flunkey
Was visiting and now they stopped writing
forgot about me and spend all day dyking

9:54 PM CST
11-28-2015

Please Don't Leave

My girl think I'm doing eight
when it's actually eighteen
She really ain't no fool
looked me up after sentencing

I keep saying eight
she nod and agree
We both know the truth
I wish I was free

I know she got a boyfriend
I keep calling her mine
In my mind we together
luckily she give me some time

Last time in prison
she visited and sent money
Held the crib and kids down
my girl strong and smart—no dummy

She told me if I go back
she was gone leave
I can feel her slipping away
at night, to God, I plead

Please let her stay
this time I'll be right
No more smoking and hanging out
I cry in my cell at night

5:45 PM CST
11-30-2015

Us and the Kids

Her perfidious smile tells the truth
Pernicious love delicately unbalanced
Tainted with visions of blue skies
Long days with us and the kids

The intimations made me think
Maybe she wants me back
Softly touching my hand
Talking about us and the kids

Our intractable romance is vexing
And my mind is wondering
Who was that, in the background, when I called?
I'm quietly pondering us and the kids

I remember morning sex
Her swallowing my grand finale
Now I barely get visits
Fading memories of us and the kids

5:22 PM CST
10-03-2015

For Our Kids

Our adulation for our children acting grown
Shouldn't adumbrate that too many won't grow old
Our expectation for our progeny ain't Harvard or Howard
Shouldn't expunge that my people choose to live like cowards
Our indulgence for our offspring committing fratricide
Shouldn't indispose parents from beating their behind
Our orientation for our babies making babies
Shouldn't obscure that they haven't rebuilt Haiti
Our undertaking for our kids because of love for them
Should unify us to fight the system until we win

3:08 PM CST
9-14-2015

Acknowledgments

This book is dedicated to all the people who have ever been forgotten, marginalized, or treated as outsiders. The challenges of life are bestowed upon us or we make choices that create them. Irrespective of how we get to an impasse, my aim is to provide the hope to see past life's difficulties and to thrive as a person who was once broken and is now whole again.

My special thanks to the people who made this book a reality: Kira Henschel, DarRen Morris, Pastor Michelle, Pastor Joe, and Mother Pat.

To all the people at the Oshkosh Correctional Institution who encouraged me: Hamid, BT, Rob, Will, and Nurse Jackie.

Finally, with a humble heart, I thank and acknowledge my supportive family: my parents, John and Barbara; my sister, Simone, my cousins, Danae and Dana; and my two special friends, Pokey and Big K.

About the Author

Jon-Darren is a man of purpose who was formed and birthed in struggle. He was born in Milwaukee, Wisconsin. He received his BA in Economics and held positions at various Fortune 500 companies.

Due to poor choices, lack of self-esteem, and neglected mental health needs, he went to prison for five years. While incarcerated, he began to write poetry and prose to provide an outlet for this thoughts and give solace during times of solitude and seemingly endless darkness.

Jon-Darren emerged renewed and enlightened to the plight of marginalized, forgotten people. His work is a reflection and commitment to all people considered "others" and is a testament to the power of love, truth, and justice.

You can contact Jon-Darren at JonDarren@yahoo.com

Printed in the USA
CPSIA information can be obtained
at www.ICGtesting.com
LVHW090110040224
770848LV00051B/916